D1527568

to: ______________________________

from: __________________________

OLD FARTS

Published by Sellers Publishing, Inc.
161 John Roberts Road, South Portland, ME 04106
Visit us at www.sellerspublishing.com • E-mail: rsp@rsvp.com

 Like Us on Facebook

Compiled by Robin Haywood.

ISBN-13: 978-1-4162-4529-2

Printed and bound in China.

10 9 8 7 6 5 4 3 2 1

OLD FARTS

THERE OUGHT TO BE A LAW...

ART BY ERIC DECETIS

SELLERS
PUBLISHING

Fart: a boring or contemptible person;
an old fart

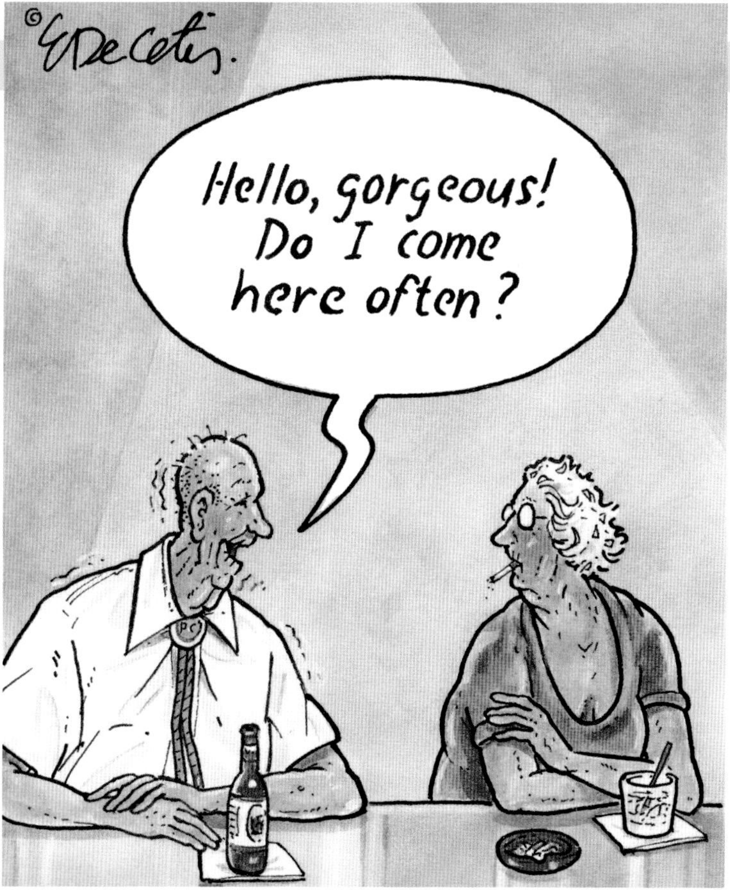
©EDeCeti.
Hello, gorgeous! Do I come here often?

Old fart: the tenth circle of Hell

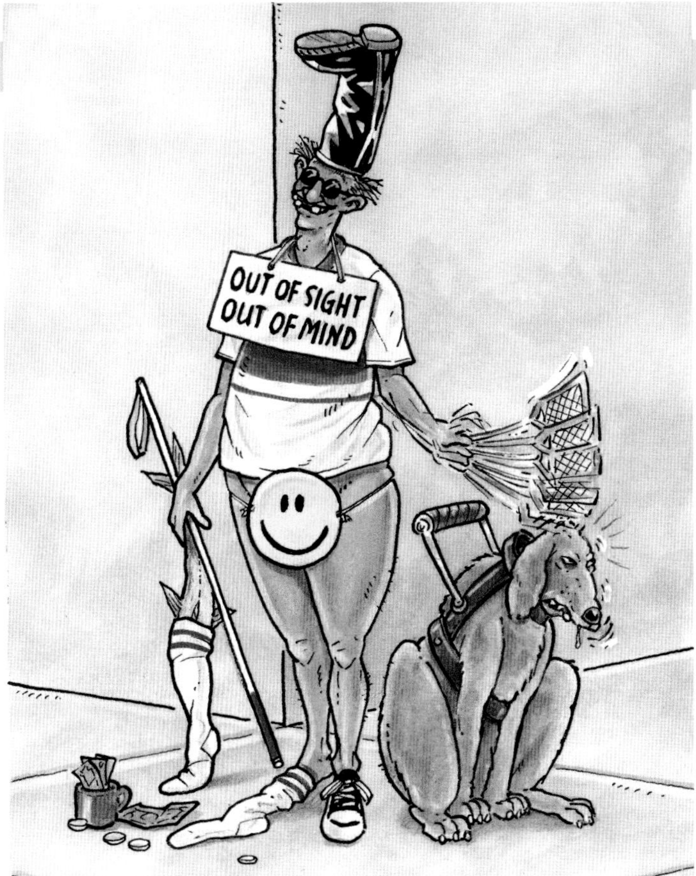
OUT OF SIGHT
OUT OF MIND

Farten (Sv): old men who behave foolishly or wander aimlessly

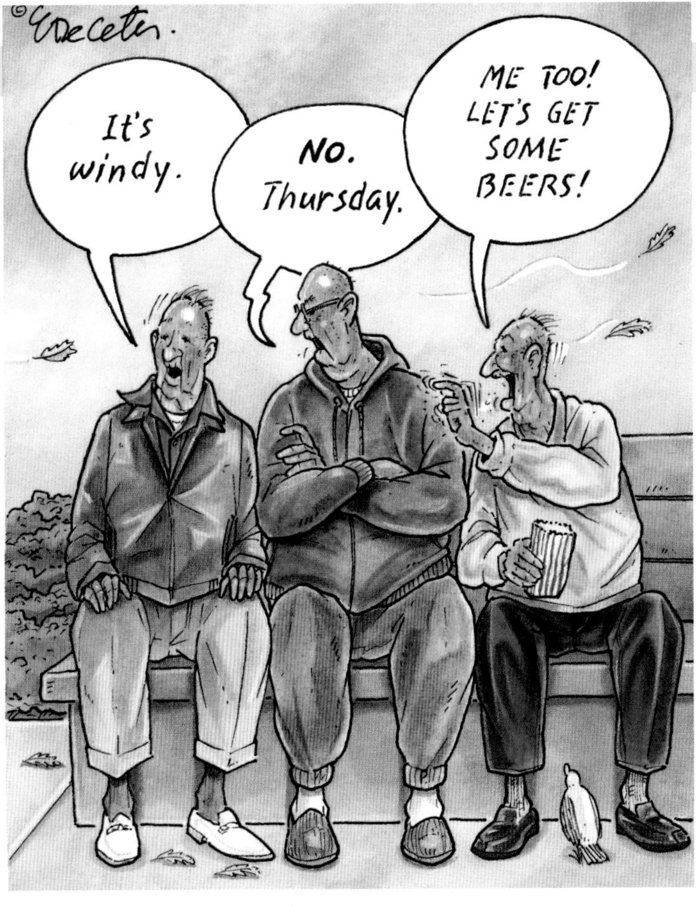
©Erdeceter.
It's windy.
No. Thursday.
ME TOO! LET'S GET SOME BEERS!

Old fart: geezer

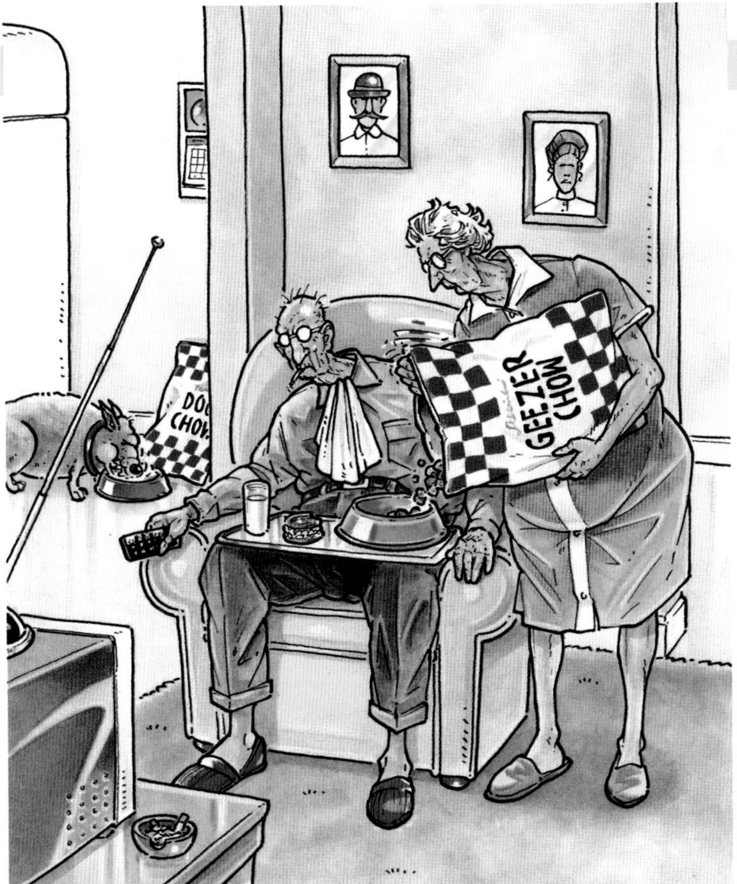
DOG CHOW
GEEZER CHOW

Geezer fashionista: a devoted follower of style

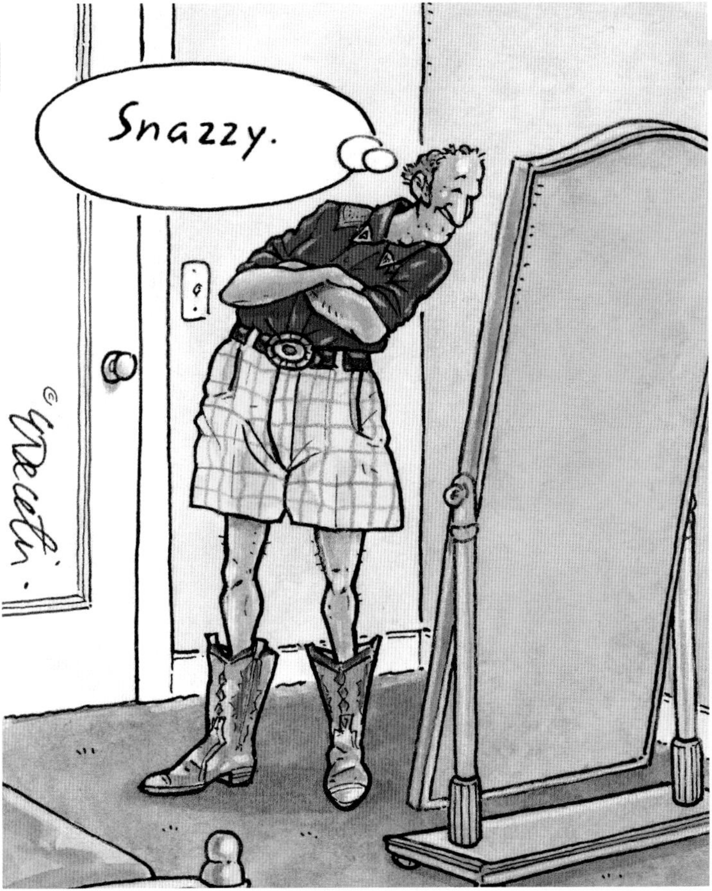
Snazzy.

Old man (Sp.): vejete

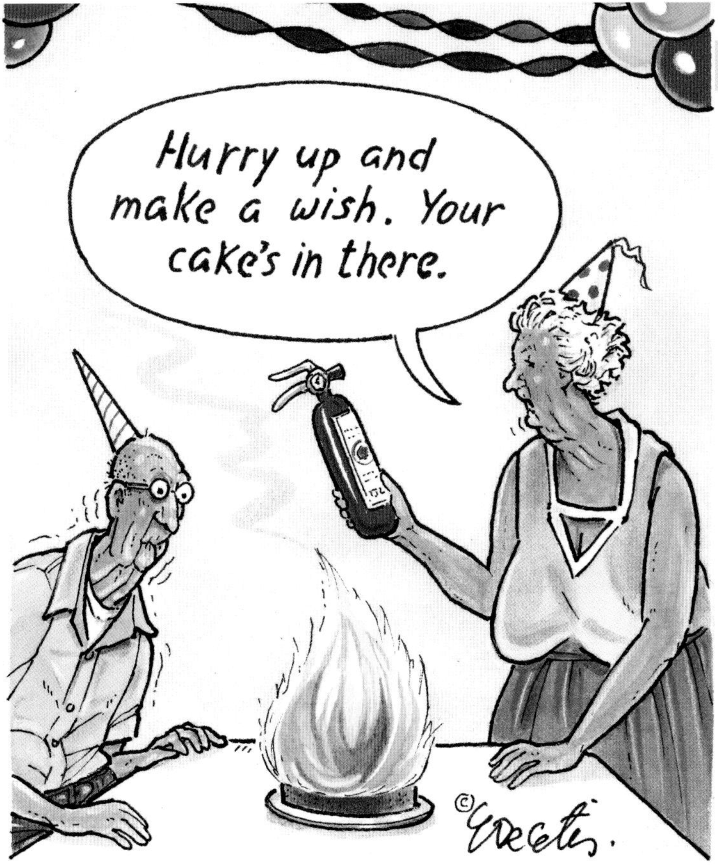
Hurry up and make a wish. Your cake's in there.
©Vreeles.

BOF: boring old fart

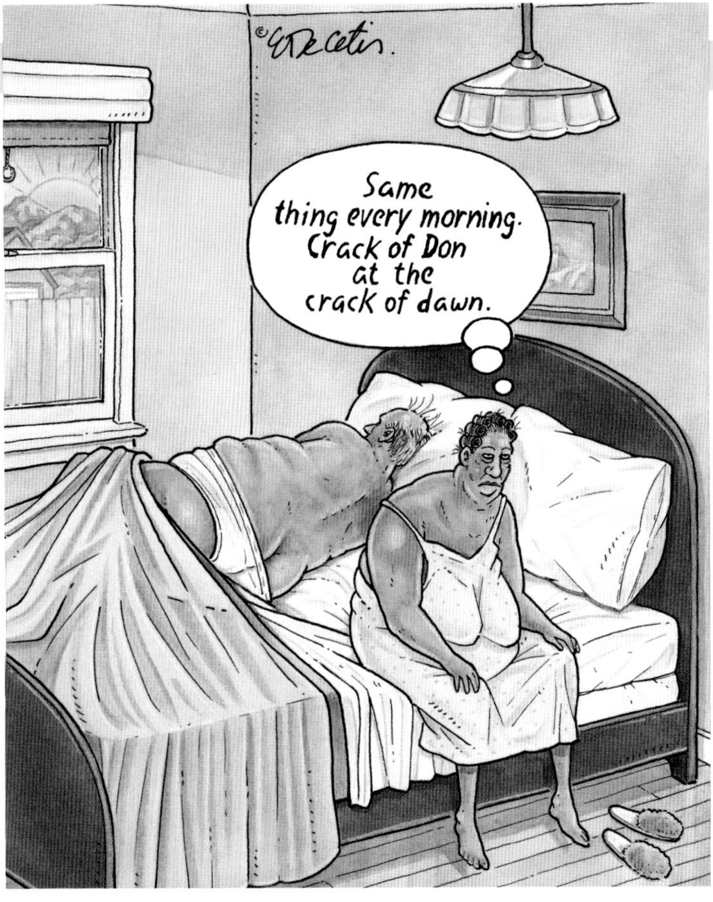
Same thing every morning. Crack of Don at the crack of dawn.

Old poop (Sp.): caca antiguo

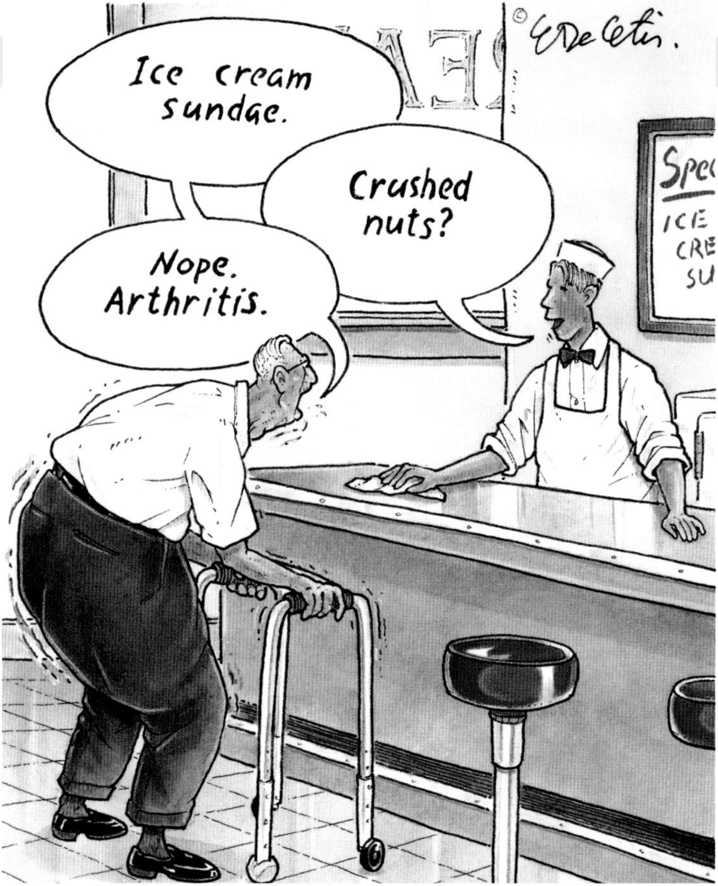
Ice cream sundae.
Crushed nuts?
Nope. Arthritis.

Geezerdom: the stage of life in which one is no longer young

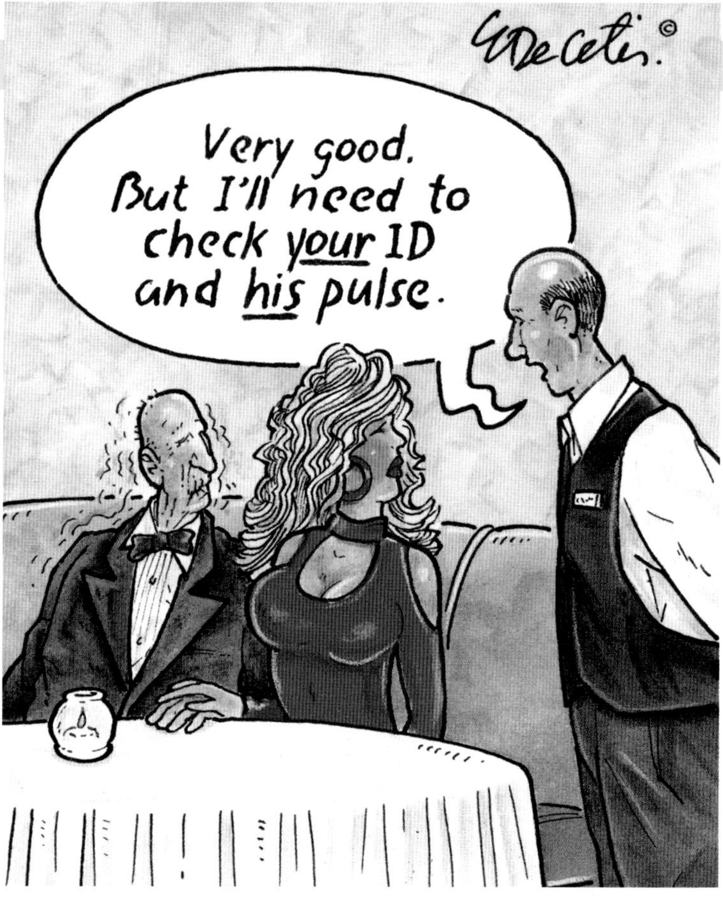
Very good.
But I'll need to check your ID and his pulse.

Old fart (Fr.): pet vieux

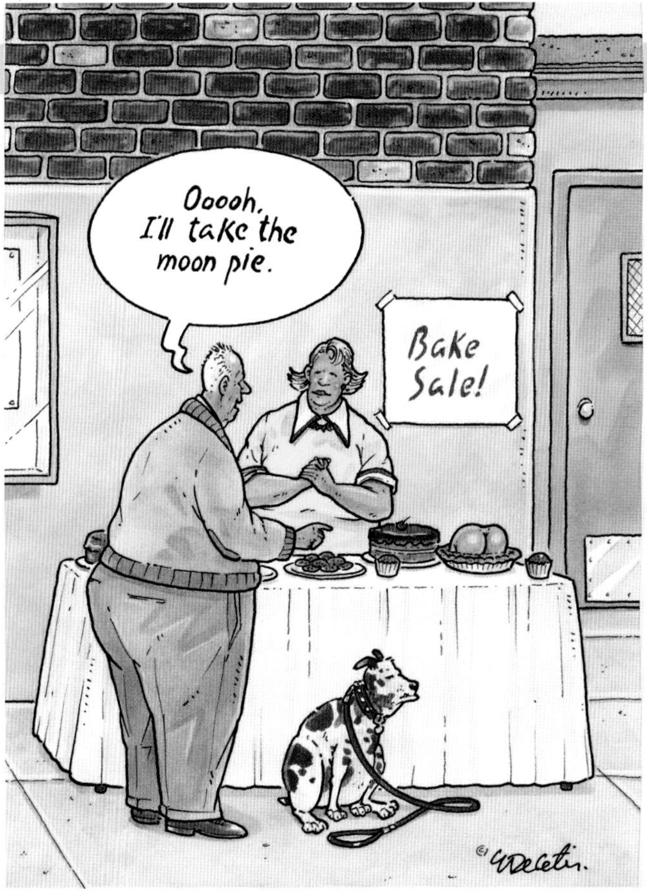
Ooooh, I'll take the moon pie.
Bake Sale!
© WDeCeti.

Old ass (Cz.): staré zadek

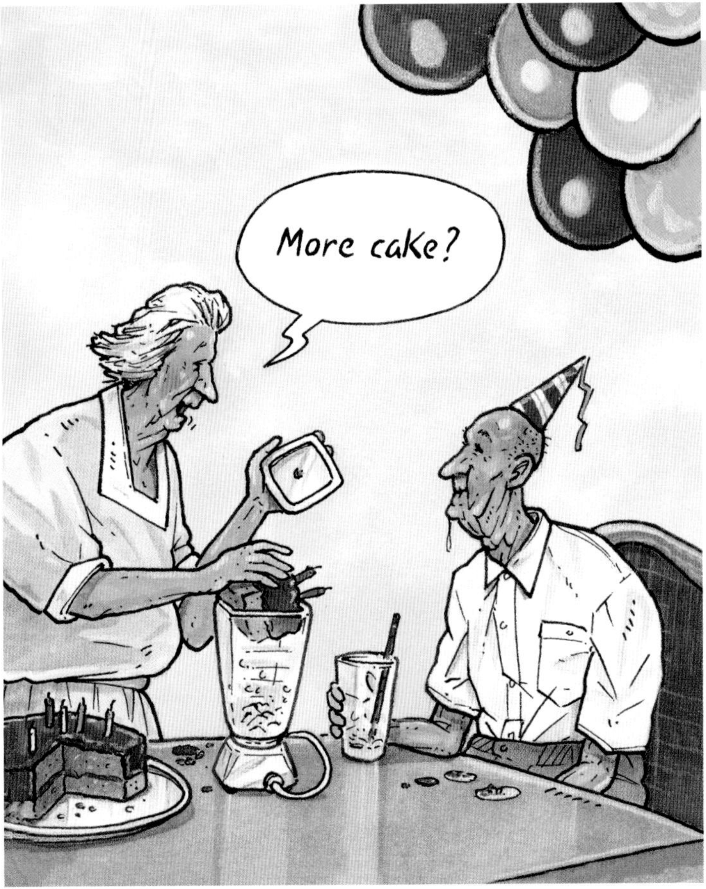
More cake?

Fart: ass thunder

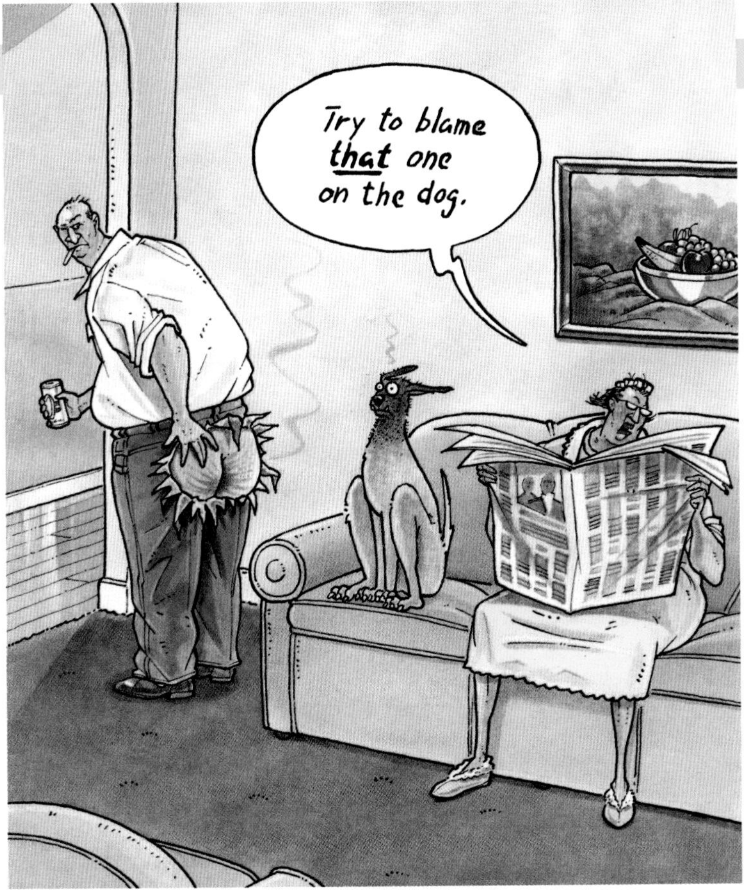
Try to blame that one on the dog.

Geezer (Norw.): gamlingen

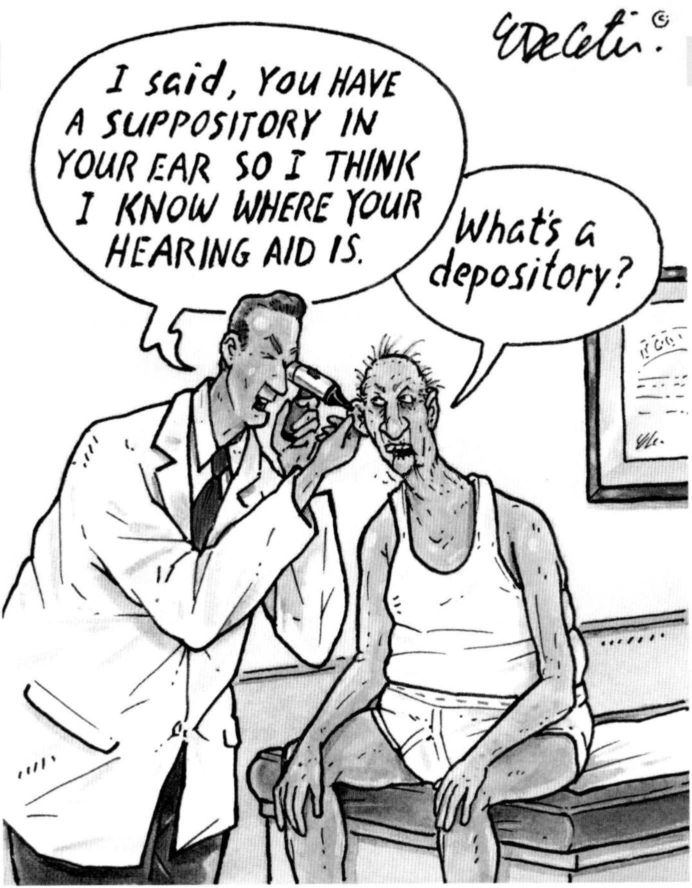
I said, YOU HAVE A SUPPOSITORY IN YOUR EAR SO I THINK I KNOW WHERE YOUR HEARING AID IS.
What's a depository?

Old fart (It.): vecchie scoreggia

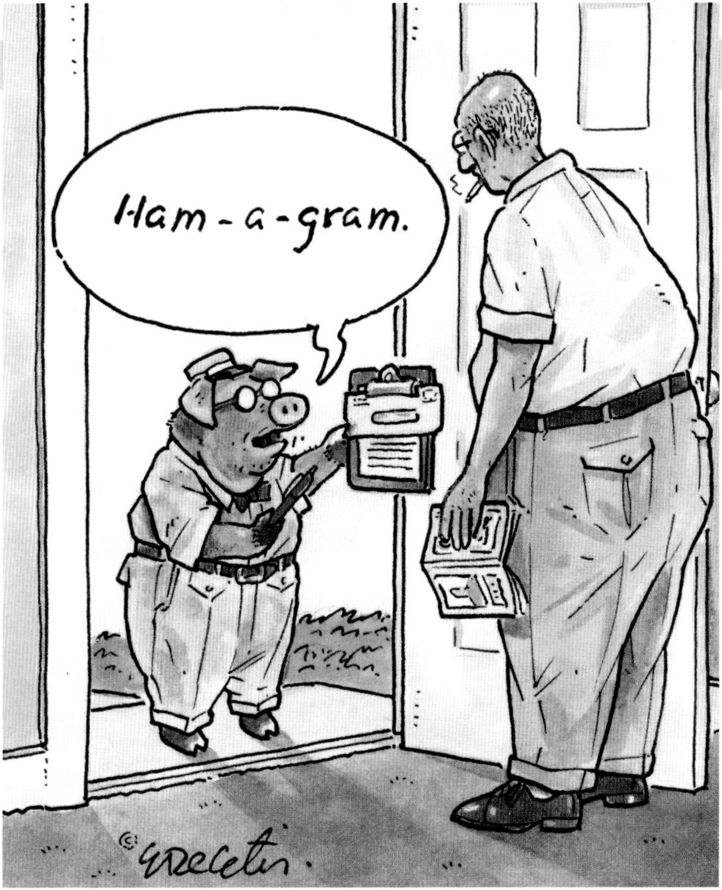
Ham-a-gram.
©Grzecen

Gramps (Turk.): dede

©GDeCetin.
How'd you know it was a hairpiece?
I think it was the chin strap.

Senior citizen (Fr.): personne âgée

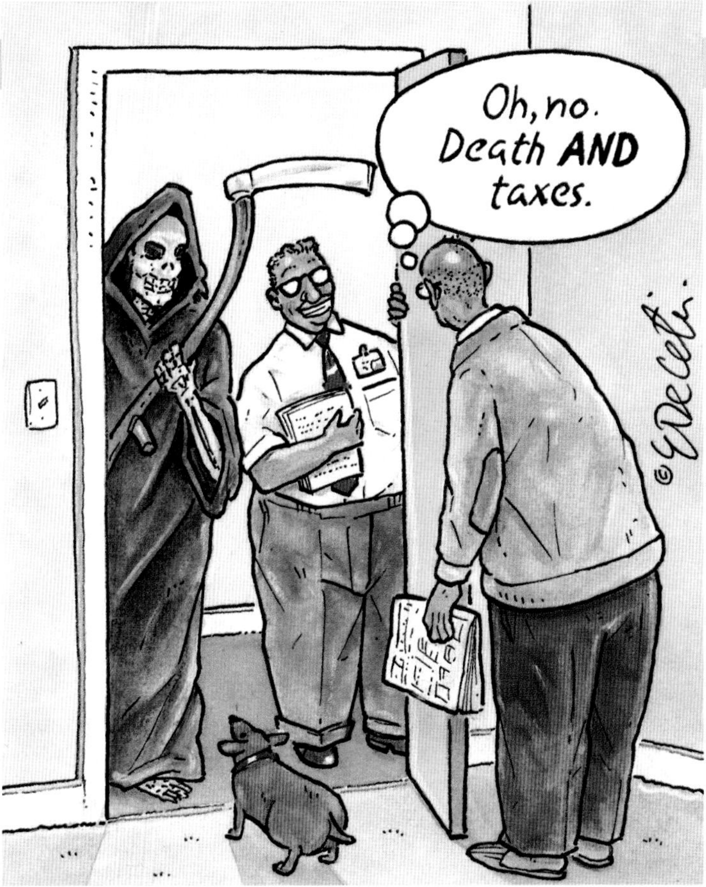
Oh, no.
Death AND
taxes.
©EDeceti

Old chap (Ger.): alter Junge

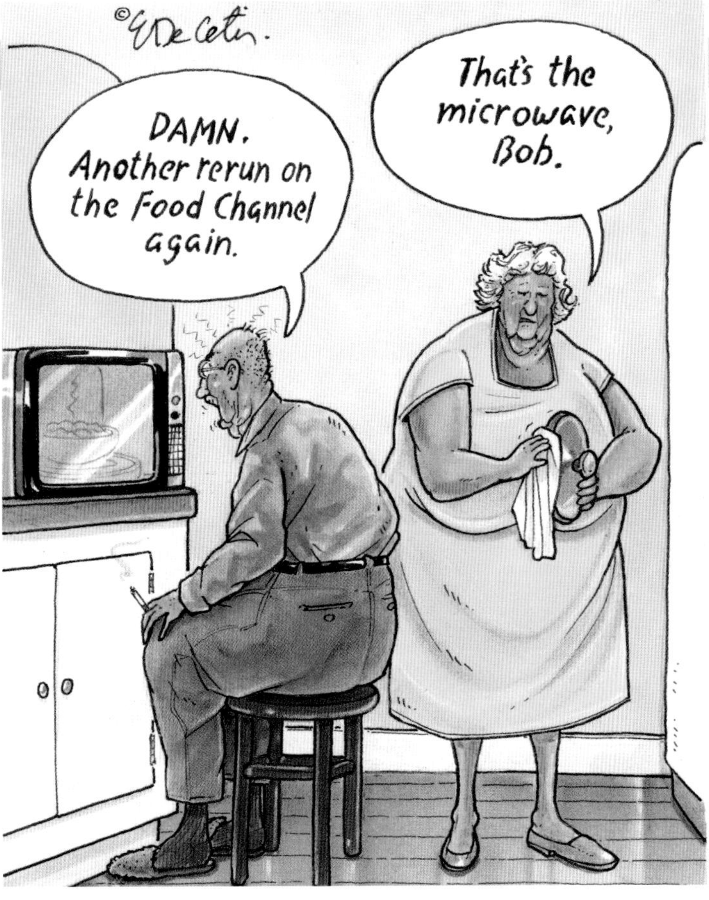
©E De Cetin.
DAMN.
Another rerun on the Food Channel again.
That's the microwave, Bob.

Fuddy-duddy: a person who has,
among other things, a saggy fanny

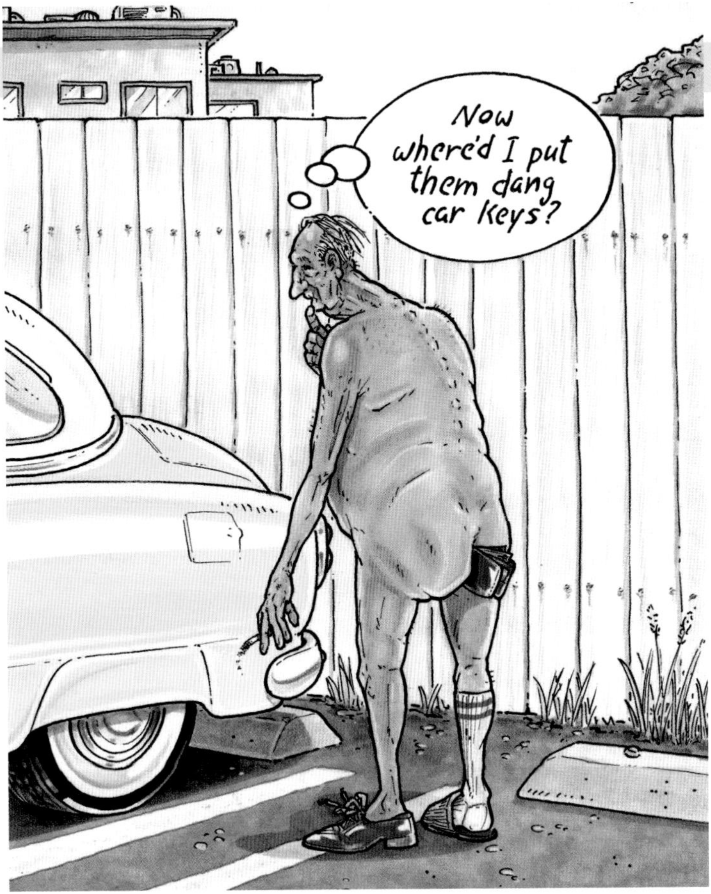
Now where'd I put them dang car keys?

Old fart: one who farts dust

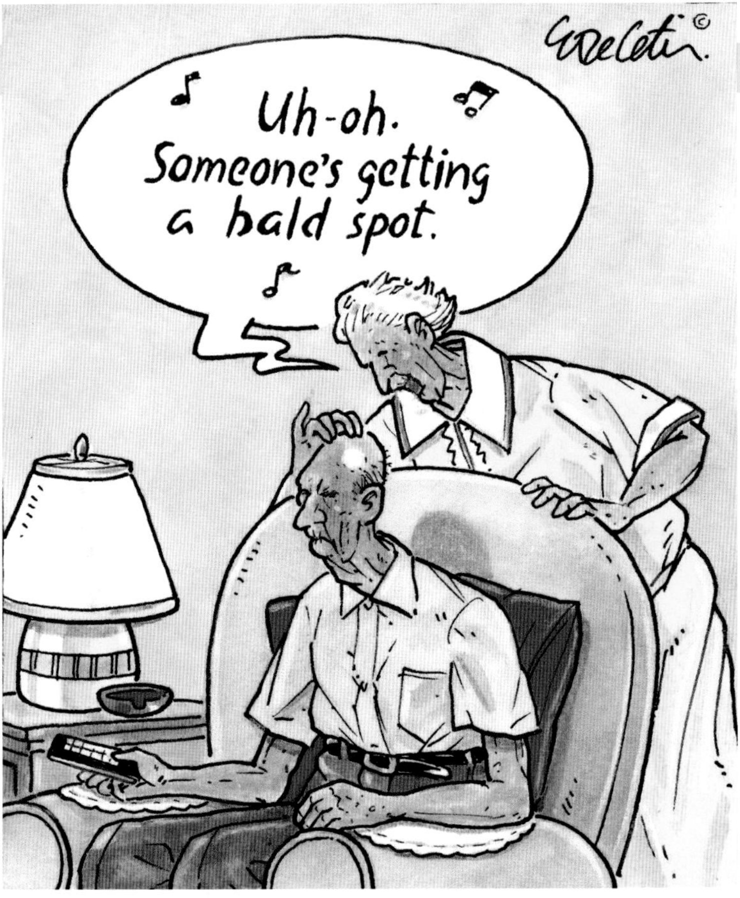
Uh-oh.
Someone's getting
a bald spot.

Senior: an older person who has lost his or her facilities

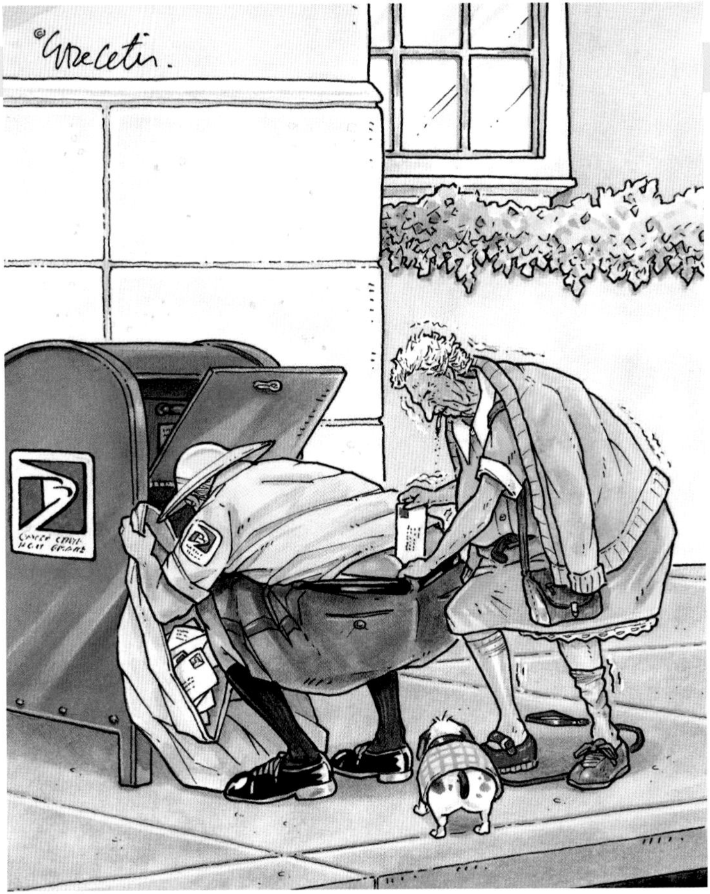
©Grecetin.

Old fogey (Turk.): eski kafali kimse

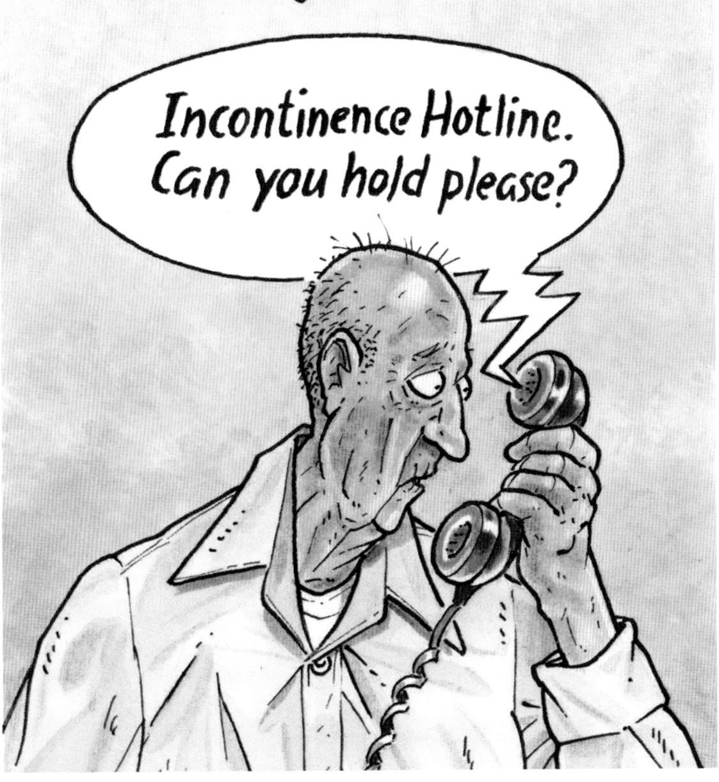
Incontinence Hotline.
Can you hold please?

Fuddy-duddy (Turk.): tutucu kimse

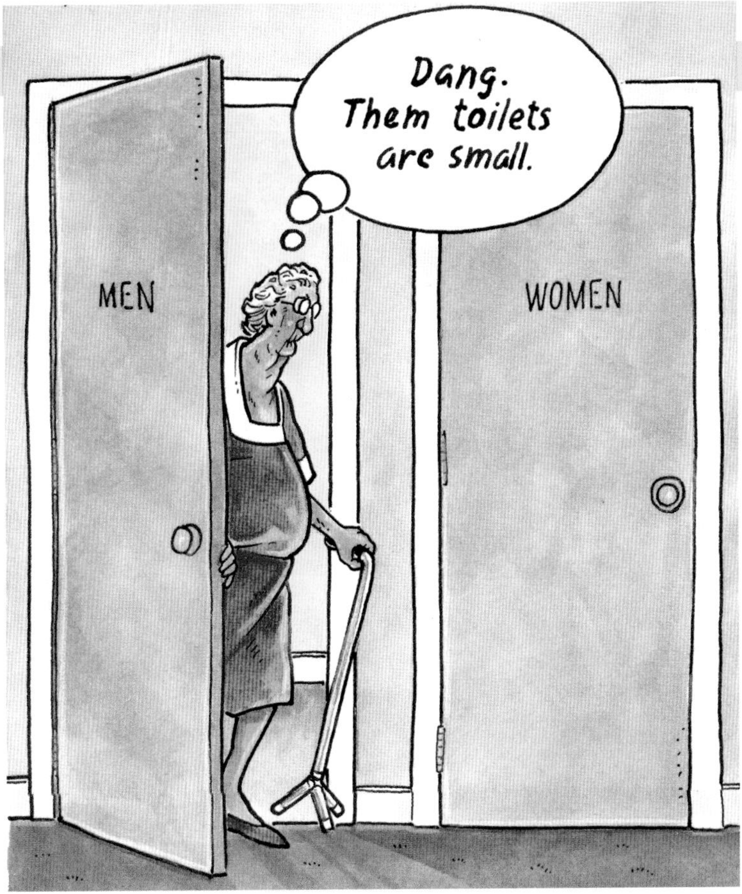
Dang.
Them toilets
are small.
MEN
WOMEN

Old fart: too old to cut the mustard

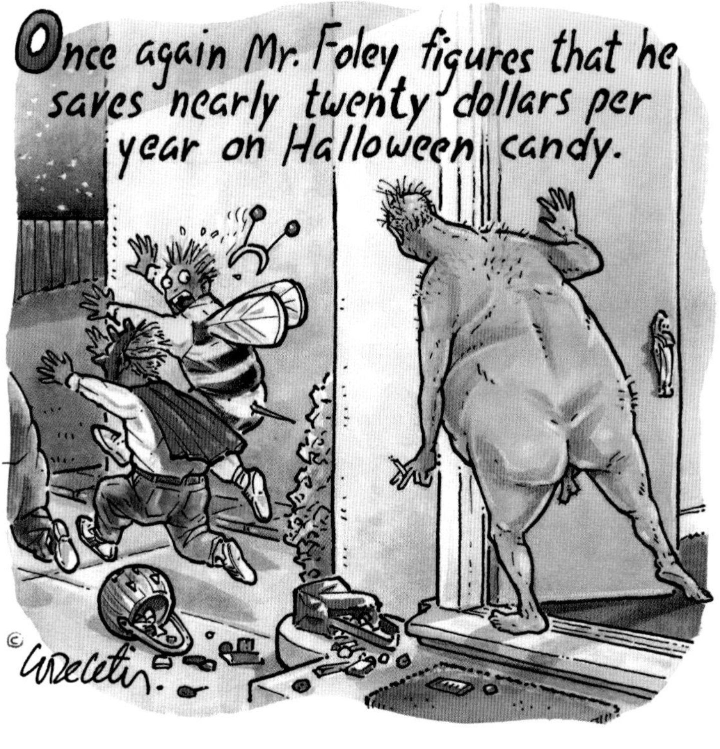
Once again Mr. Foley figures that he saves nearly twenty dollars per year on Halloween candy.

Stage of life (Port.): geriátrica

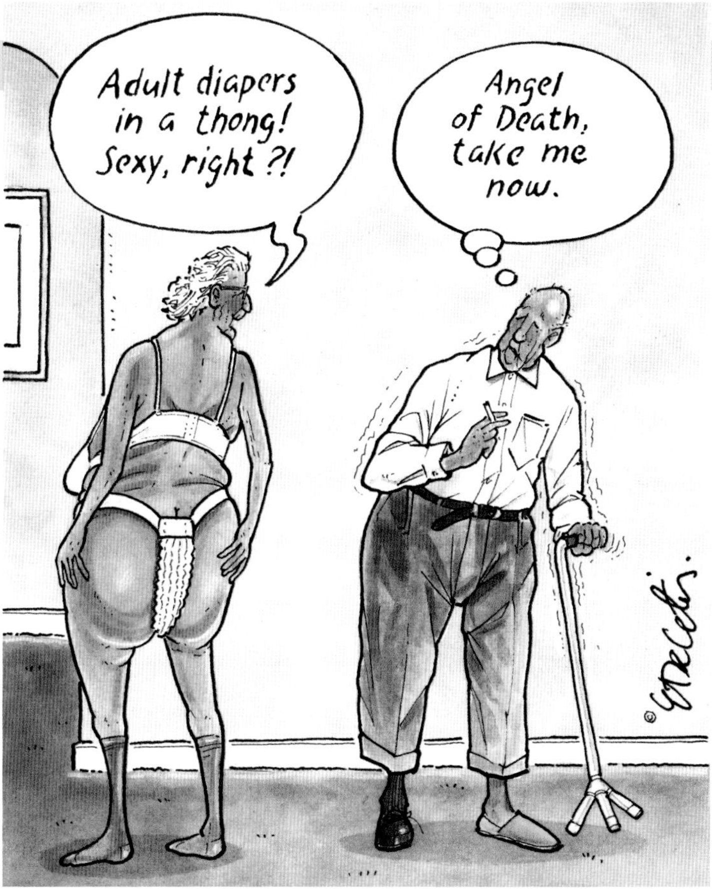
Adult diapers in a thong! Sexy, right ?!
Angel of Death, take me now.
© DeCeCo

Old poop (Fr.): caca vieux

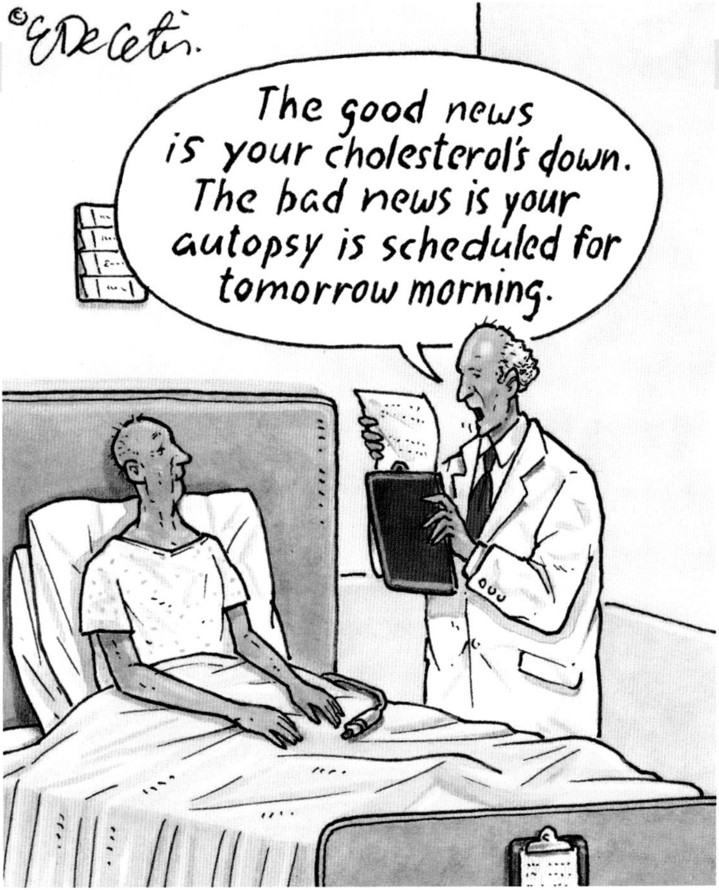
The good news is your cholesterol's down. The bad news is your autopsy is scheduled for tomorrow morning.

Senior moment: can't remember something that's very obvious

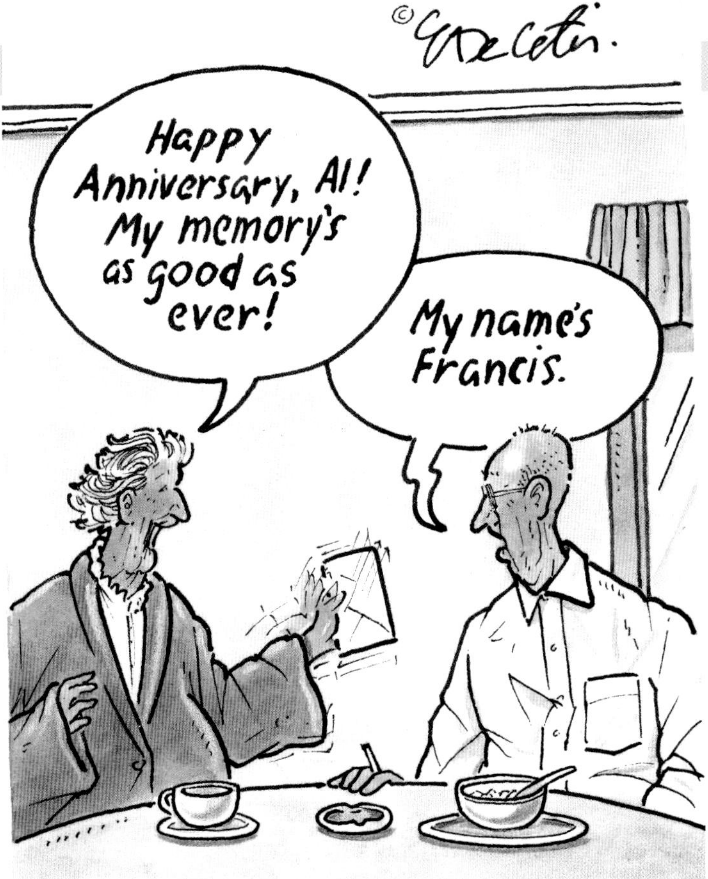
©
Happy Anniversary, Al! My memory's as good as ever!
My name's Francis.

Codger (Ger.): kauz

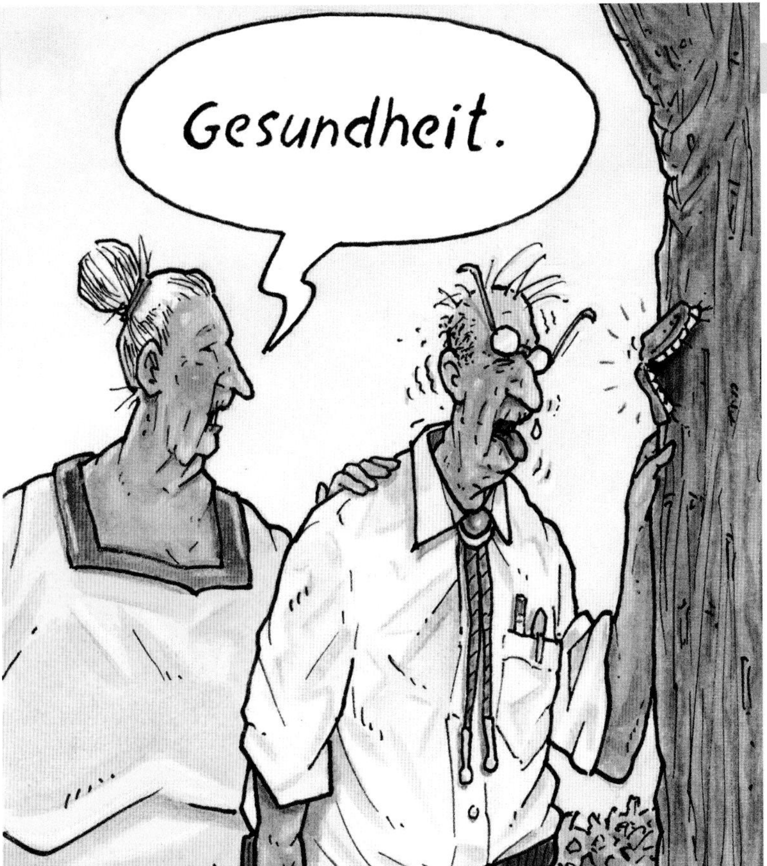
Gesundheit.

Baldation: a form of baldness where there is still some hair

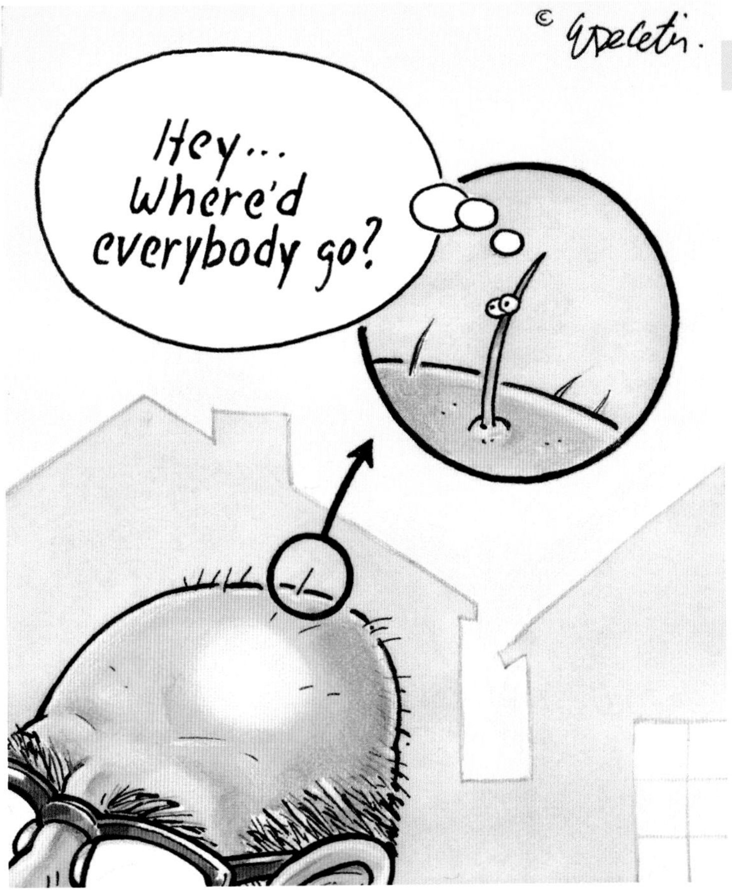
© Eseleti.
Hey...
Where'd
everybody go?

Duffer: someone in an addle-brained stage of life

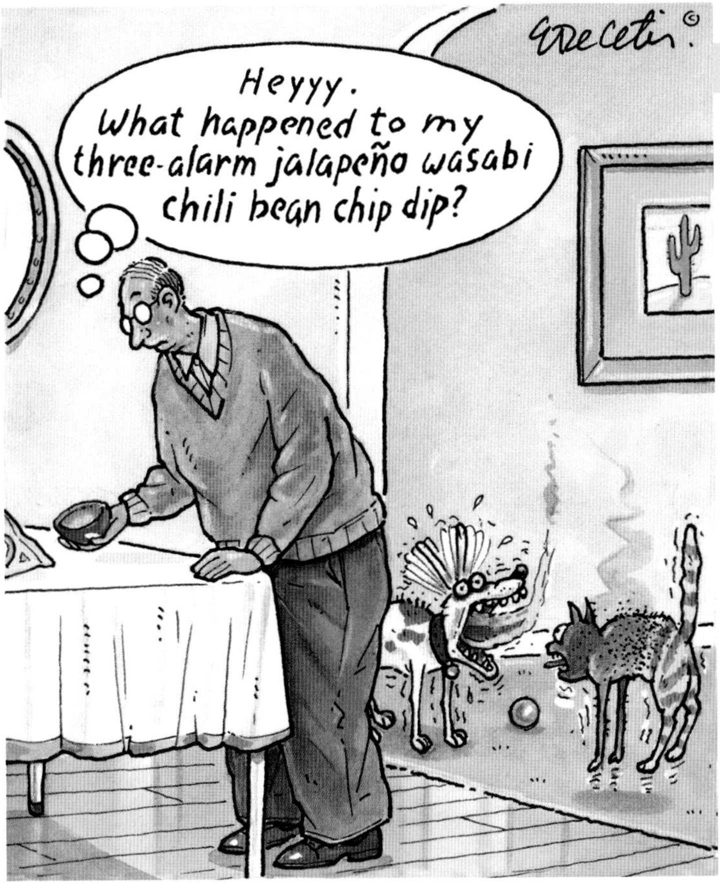
Heyyy.
What happened to my three-alarm jalapeño wasabi chili bean chip dip?

Vogueish old coot: one who is influenced by popular styles

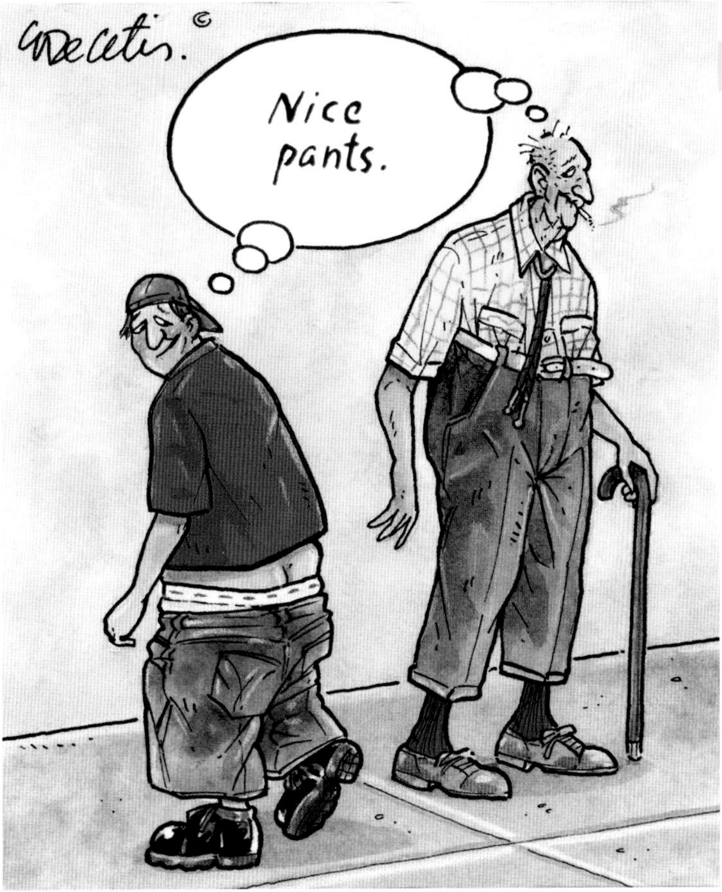
Nice
pants.